DIY Publishing Toolkit

Contents

V GETTING YOUR BOOK INTO PEOPLE'S HANDS: PLANS FOR DISTRIBUTION

VI TELLING PEOPLE ABOUT YOUR BOOK: MARKETING

VII APPENDICES: STUFF IT'S GOOD TO KNOW

Acknowledgments

We acknowledge the traditional owners of the land where we work and write. The University of Melbourne is located on the unceded lands of the Wurundjeri Woi Wurrung people, and the University of Queensland is located on the unceded lands of the Jagera, Yugara/Yugarapul, and Turrbal peoples. We pay our respects to their Elders, past and present.

We also acknowledge the traditional owners of the lands where we conducted interviews and workshops that have led to the production of this guide. Ayr is located on the lands of the Bindal and Juru People, Winton on the lands of the Koa people, Alice Springs/Mparntwe on the lands of the Arrernte people, and Broken Hill on the lands of the Wilyakali people.

This toolkit arises from a research project that was funded by the Australian government through the Australian Research Council's Linkage scheme (LP210300666), with contributions from seven partners in addition to the University of Melbourne and the University of Queensland: Alice Springs Town Council, Broken Hill Council , Booktopia, Burdekin Shire Council, Busybird Publishing, the Small Press Network, and Winton City Council. We are grateful for their support.

Thank you to the research assistants for this project, Caitlin Parker and Roseleigh Priest, who provided invaluable coordination and research support. Thanks to Louisa Preston and Teaka Williams for support with cover design, and to Caitlin Parker (again) for logo design. We are grateful to IngramSpark, who supported the project by providing a generous discount for printing this toolkit.

And a huge thank you to all our interviewees, workshop participants, and everyone across Australia who reached out because they were interested in this project, and because they believe in the importance of sharing stories through making books.

Introduction

Welcome to the DIY Publishing Toolkit. Writing and publishing a book is one of the most satisfying creative activities there is, and it's more accessible than ever. Putting together your own book has always been possible, but new digital technologies are available that can make some steps faster, cheaper and easier. There are also new ways to outsource some parts of publishing while keeping creative control over others. This guide aims to give you the information you need to write and publish your own book the way that you want to, whether that's the story of your life, a poetry collection, a children's book, or something else.

In this guide, you'll find advice and information on everything from choosing a printer to designing a cover. Depending on your motivations for publishing, you might like to read the sections on marketing and selling your book, or on creating beautiful objects that your friends and family will cherish. You can dip in and out of this toolkit and read the sections in any order.

This guide is the outcome of years of publishing experience from the authors and the people we've worked with. The four authors – Beth Driscoll, Kim Wilkins, Alexandra Dane, and Sandra Phillips – are academics who teach and research book publishing at the University of Melbourne and the University of Queensland. Sandra has also worked as a publisher and editor, at IAD and Magabala Books, and Kim is also a fiction writer who has published over 30 novels. Between us, we have published 85 academic articles, 10 academic books, and taught thousands of students about writing and publishing.

The four of us came together in 2023 for a research project, Community Publishing in Regional Australia. Publishing has traditionally been concentrated in the capital cities where multinational companies are based, but we wanted to raise the profile of the DIY publishing activities happening outside of major cities. We partnered with seven organisations. Three industry groups had an interest in learning more about and meeting the needs of DIY publishers: Booktopia, an online retailer that is an Australian alternative to Amazon, Busybird Publishing, a company that supports writers to make books, and Small Press Network, a peak body for small publishers in Australia. We also partnered with councils in four Australian towns – Alice Springs/Mparntwe, Broken Hill, Winton and Ayr – and conducted interviews and workshops with local writers in each place. You'll find some of their publishing stories and insights throughout this guide.

So, onto the DIY Publishing Toolkit! Pick a section, get started, and happy publishing.

I

GETTING INTO PUBLISHING

1

Start here: Your idea for a book

You are probably here because you already have an idea for a book. Maybe you are a born storyteller and your family and friends are always telling you to write it down. Maybe you have been active in a local history group and think you have enough stories to compile into a book. Maybe you want to set the record straight or give your perspective on a public issue. Or maybe you want to write a made-up story about magicians, murders, or mighty passions.

It's good to understand the difference between non-fiction and fiction, because this is a really important distinction in publishing. Non-fiction stories are about things that really happened: to you, to a relative, in history, and so on. How faithful to the facts non-fiction has to be is a matter of style. Lots of memoirs and histories are very creatively told.

Rainie Gillies' idea for her book Winton, Working and
Wags came from the tea and coffee mornings that she
started hosting during COVID. Rainie's friends would
gather and catch up on life in the town of Winton and
share stories from their past. One of the people who
would attend the coffee mornings was Jeff Close, who
runs Spur 'n Eight publishing. Jeff urged Rainie to
write down her stories of Winton and of her life in
the region, and together they published these stories
into a book. Winton, Working and Wags, which now has
a second edition, is a popular record of the social
history of Winton.

Fiction stories are about things that didn't really happen, or
jump off creatively from something that did really happen.
There are lots of different genres of fiction, including crime,
romance, historical, and so on.

When you're developing your book idea, have a think about
who it's for. Who would like to read it? When and where would
they like to read it? And where would they be most likely to find
it? In a bookstore? Online? At an agricultural fair? Thinking
about who the book is for can help focus you while you are
writing or editing. If you are stuck, you can ask what would
your ideal reader like to read?

Rose Siva's children's fiction about dinosaurs is
inspired by her work as a fossil hunter and her
background in education. 'I know that engaging kids
in good material is the first key to actually getting
them to read. And every kid loves dinosaurs, so here
I had, in this wonderful situation, I've got material

```
that I can wrap fiction around fact, and I can write.
And I know how to write books that kids like reading.'
```

One other really important thing to think about is whose story you're telling, and are you the right person to tell it. If you write things about real people or groups, you could seriously upset somebody or it could even be illegal. A good rule of thumb is to ask for permission if you want to recount an individual's story, or their relatives if that person is no longer alive. There are plenty of other ways to make sure that you aren't taking credit for a story that's not your own. You could co-write the story, offer to share royalties, or turn it into a community project that lots of people can contribute to. Being careful about ownership goes for illustrations too. If you're unsure, you can contact your state writing organisation, who may be able to offer advice or direct you to resources.

2

Reasons to publish a book: Keep your motivation high!

'It was creative expression and it was just a huge privilege to see it bound in a book, in print.' — Annette Herd, author of We Live, We Die

There are plenty of good reasons to write and publish a book. Writing creatively, while sometimes challenging, can also be a lot of fun. It gives you a chance to express what you've seen or felt or imagined. There's nothing more satisfying than seeing the page count grow, or to write 'the end', or to hold a published copy of your work in your hands. That came out of your head! But publishing a book is also great to pass on your wisdom and stories to other people.

> 'I wrote, originally, for my family, to let them know
> what I went through growing up in this country' —
> John Spencer, author of Both Sides of the Fence

If you know something, why not tell readers about it? It might make their lives better, or it might mean that your knowledge survives into the future.

> 'I've always been fascinated by history, so the thing
> that drives me is recording history ... I try to
> encourage books or help co-write books and things
> that are recording our history ... That is ours and
> it's up to us to nurture that, record it, pass it
> on.' - Jeff Close, Spur N Eight Publishing

You might even make some money out of a book. Imagine if your local writers group compiled a pretty hardcover book full of short stories. You could sell them at a writers festival or in the newsagent, and make a small income to support your writing workshops.

If you are finding it tough going, stuck in edits or trying to figure out what font to use, remind yourself why you're doing this. And imagine that amazing moment when the box of your books arrives, and you can start giving them to friends.

> 'My book was emotionally led, which is something that
> can carry you along when you think you can't do it.
> Your emotions will just keep you going...with this
> book, I was driven by my family history and my family

story.' - Sonya Bradley-Shoyer, author of Come...Walk
With Me

'I was impressed just to publish one book and now I
look back and I think, Lord, how did you do that? I'm
really chuffed with myself for every single thing I
do. It's exciting to write something. It's exciting
to hear when someone actually reads it and they
actually like it. You think, I just got four stars.
And that's exciting that someone actually enjoyed
something I did. But also, it's an outlet. It's a
creative outlet for me. And I'm doing what I love. '
- Kathleen Ryder, author of A Fling with the Flying
Doctor

Take some time to reflect on why you want to write and publish
a book. Ask your friends and family if they think it's a good
idea. They might get so excited that they become your biggest
supporter as you face the challenges ahead.

3

Get ready to be entrepreneurial

In traditional publishing, you send your manuscript to a publisher, they agree to publish it, and that's pretty much your job done. While the publisher's editorial process might require you to do some re-writes, the publishing house will then drive publication.

For DIY publishing, you need to be both a writer and an entrepreneur who manages and directs everything to do with your book. It's like setting up as a small business or sole trader. So while a lot of writers might feel like publishing begins once there's a manuscript ready, if you're DIY Publishing it's never too early to be thinking about the practical aspects of your project.

```
'I think I prefer to contribute to the marketing and
all that. I've been more than happy to go and do all
the talks and all that, but I don't want to have that
responsibility where I have to run a whole show.' -
Annette Herd, author of We Live, We Die
```

DIY publishing involves a lot of different activities beyond writing: you're also responsible for budgeting, design, printing, storing and distributing the copies. This calls for skills from wrangling documents and online portals to business administration. Think of it as project managing your own book. It is extra effort, but you get creative control over the finished product, and you get to keep any potential profit from sales of the book.

> 'So the reason I published myself: originally, I wasn't going to, I was going to send it to everybody, and then I thought, why should I? I did everything. I mean, I wrote it. I found an editor, I found a book cover designer. I had it formatted. I did all of that on my own. Nobody was there making me coffee and patting me on the back and propping me up. So why then should I give half of my money to other people?'
> Kathleen Ryder, author of A Fling with the Flying Doctor

Being the project manager doesn't mean you have to do absolutely everything yourself. You might ask friends or hire people or services to do some of the work for you. If you decide to work with freelancers for some or all tasks (such as cover design or copy editing), you pay a fee and keep copyright, creative control, and all potential profit from sales. You might decide to work with an author services company that packages together a number of services; if so, do make sure that you're working with a reputable company that has competitive and transparent pricing (read more in Chapter 21).

```
'I found a crowd called IngramSpark. Fabulous site,
fabulous how-to guides, fabulous all the way through
but you really have to put in the hours to learn how
to do it. Whereas if you go to a publisher you just
go, here it is, take it away, you do it. You do the
page layout. I don't care; it's all going to happen.
When you do Indie publishing you've actually got to
be aware of all these things yourself: the amount of
white space, the chapter layout....You can pay
somebody else to do it and I certainly did with the
cover' - Rose Siva, author of DINOCROC: A Hunt for
Ancient Crocodiles
```

A tip: buy a special notebook that you use only to keep notes and ideas about your publishing journey. That way, when you do it all again, it's easy to find all the information you need. Also, it's a great excuse to buy stationery!

Perhaps you're not sure if you do want to be an entrepreneur and project manager. Maybe your strengths and interests lie elsewhere? Try the decision tree below to clarify your preferred approach

4

Decision tree: What kind of publishing is best for you?

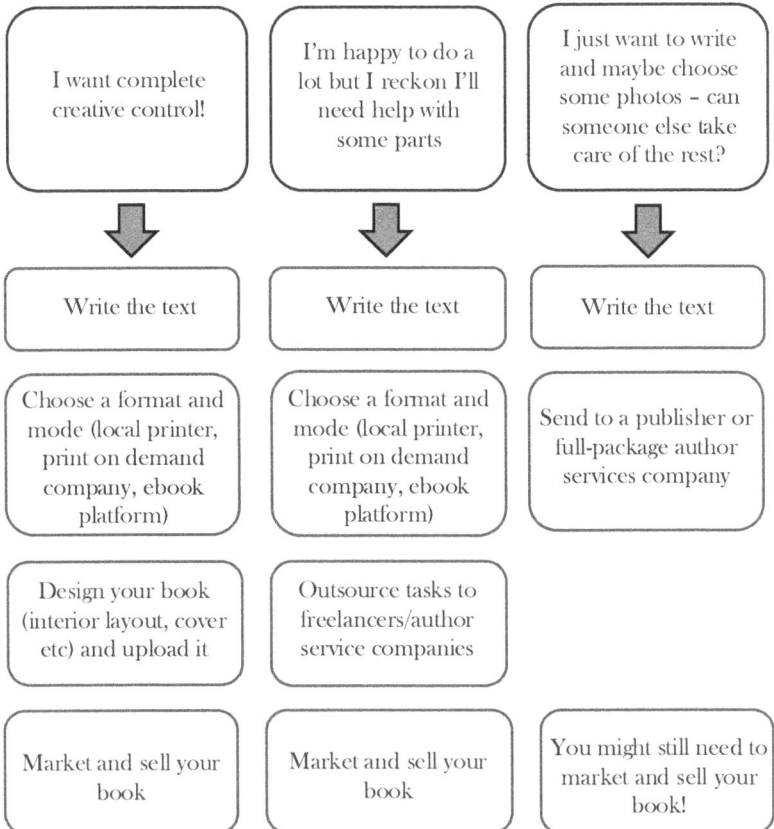

I want complete creative control!	I'm happy to do a lot but I reckon I'll need help with some parts	I just want to write and maybe choose some photos – can someone else take care of the rest?
↓	↓	↓
Write the text	Write the text	Write the text
Choose a format and mode (local printer, print on demand company, ebook platform)	Choose a format and mode (local printer, print on demand company, ebook platform)	Send to a publisher or full-package author services company
Design your book (interior layout, cover etc) and upload it	Outsource tasks to freelancers/author service companies	
Market and sell your book	Market and sell your book	You might still need to market and sell your book!

5

You don't have to do it alone

Believe it or not, there are lots of people who write and publish books; with the ease of online services, there are more than ever. If you are feeling overwhelmed or isolated, you could reach out to a writers group for friendship, networking, and to share ideas.

Most states have a writers centre, which can refer you to a local group for in-person meetings. Just google your state name and "writers centre". There are also online writers groups that are not limited by where you live. Romance writers have thriving online communities, for example. Facebook is a great place to search for them, and you can find them by searching for terms such as "self-publishing", "independent publishing", "writing support", and so on. There are also websites where you can write and publish stories online like Wattpad, Inkitt, and Archive of our Own, depending on your genre and your interests.

II

WORDS AND PICTURES: THE CONTENT OF YOUR BOOK

6

Writing your book

Writing a book is a matter of putting one word after another until it's done. For something that sounds simple, it can be incredibly hard! People who have been writing their whole lives—journalists, storytellers, avid childhood readers who filled notebooks with wild tales—might find it a little easier, but generally speaking, writing a book is tough going at least some of the time. Here's a few ways to make it easier, or at least make it feel more do-able.

Have an ally. That ally can be a co-writer, where you take turns to write sections; or another writer who's working on their own project and will swap pages with you; or a loved one who can encourage you to set goals and remind you to meet them. You can have a whole army of allies if you join a writing group, and these can be in person or online. More than half of the work in writing a book is just showing up consistently until it's done. That's hard to do alone.

```
Fae Le Frizz lives and writes in remote outback
Queensland, and gets support from an online writing
group. 'I can just hop on there and they'll be like,
"Oh, how's your day going?" ... And then someone will
go, "Right, okay, we're going to write for 25
minutes. We're going to write for half an hour...
make sure everyone's got their drink or their tea or
whatever."'
```

Set reasonable goals. Finding the time to write can be about more than setting aside an hour a day (though that is a great idea if you can). If you have children, wait until they're back in school before starting a writing marathon; if they're really small, you might have to stick to reading and research until they're ready to be with a babysitter.

You might have busy periods in your job, seasonal work that must be done, or community obligations to fulfill. Writing has an ebb and flow. Find the best times to flow and plan to get work done then.

Know what you want the finished book to look like. How long do you think it should be (an easy way to figure it out is to find other books like yours and work out how long they are: one page of text is about 300 words)? Does it need illustrations or photographs? Think about a catchy title, what kind of cover image would draw attention, and if it needs headings or chapters inside to structure it.

You can write a book from first page to last page, or you can write it out of order and stitch it together later. You can plan every chapter and section in advance, or you can make it up as you go along. There are lots of different ways to approach it, so choose a way that suits you and start writing.

7

The three different types of editing

Once you've finished the first draft and written 'the end', it's time to celebrate. Then it's time to edit. If you can, let the book sit for a few weeks before you think about editing it. It's best to edit with fresh eyes.

In the publishing industry, there are three kinds of editing. Structural editing for the big picture, copy-editing for better writing, and proofreading to pick up errors. Some of these you can do yourself, and some are better if you get outside help.

8

The big picture edit: Structural editing

The first type of editing is called "structural" editing. This is a big picture edit that takes in the overall structure of the book and asks questions such as:

FICTION

- Do the characters behave consistently, even as they are changed by the story?
- Does the pace flow from beginning to middle to end with rising tension?
- Is there a balanced mix of action, dialogue, and description?

NONFICTION

- Is the structure sensible and easy to follow?
- Are there any long or uninteresting parts or repetitions that can be cut to make the book engaging to read?

You can do this yourself by mapping out the book in a table, section by section, and thinking about each part individually and where it fits in the whole. In fact, making a book map is often all you need to do to find structural problems. They tend to stand out when you take the birds eye view. You can also ask one of your allies to read the book for you just to get first impressions of how it flows. What did they enjoy? When did they get bored? Were they satisfied with the ending? Or you can pay a structural editor, which may cost a few thousand dollars.

'One of my fan fiction friends lives over in Perth. I reached out to him because he's also an author. I'm like, "Hey look, would you be interested in beta reading this novel for me? I know Australiana is not your thing and I know YA isn't quite what you're after, but could you have a look?" And he was like, "Yep. So long as you do the same for mine." I said, deal. No worries.' — Grace Elliott, author of A Spot of Bother (as Fae le Friz)

9

Making the book read better: Copy-editing

The second type of editing is called "copy-editing" or sometimes "line editing". That's when an editor will look at the words and sentences you use and make sure they that are clear, but also that they are as well-expressed as they can be for the genre. A copy-edit improves the reading experience on a line-by-line level. This is the hardest edit to do yourself and it's a lot to ask a friend. Be careful, though: some people will say they are giving you a copy-edit when they are really only doing a proofread (see below). Make sure you ask whether they will be improving the writing or just looking for errors.

Also, depending on your genre and your goals for your book, you might feel you don't need a copy edit. Perhaps this is your life story, and you are just telling it 'as it is' in your voice. In such cases, a proofread may be all you need. If you do decide to pay for a copy edit, get a range of quotes and make sure you know exactly what you're paying for.

10

Finding and fixing errors: Proofreading

The third level of editing is the proofread. This is a careful read of the whole book specifically to look for mistakes and typos. You can usually do this, but you have to be slow and careful. If that doesn't sound like you, there are lots of freelance proofreaders in the world. If you know a friend who reads a lot, or even a school teacher, you could ask them to proofread. All they need is a good vocabulary and an eye for detail.

If you are going to edit your own work, look for a book or another resource that can give you some tips. We can recommend *The Art of Memoir* by Mary Karr, *Bird by Bird* by Anne Lamott, and *Self-Editing for Fiction Writers* by Renni Browne and Dave King. Brian Fry has a website about copyediting, and Masterclass has a course on editing poetry. The Independent Author Alliance also has editing advice for self-publishing authors.

11

Photos, drawings and diagrams

A lot of people like to put visual material in their books: photographs, illustrations and drawings, perhaps even diagrams. There are a few considerations about pictures to get your head around, and you should think through these and decide whether you really *need* them.

First, where will you source them? Do you have access to your own photographs? Or are you an artist as well as a writer, who can produce beautiful drawings? If you can't supply these yourself, you'll have to find them elsewhere and there may be copyright considerations or payments due to companies or individuals who supply them.

Second, adding pictures usually means adding cost and complexity to publishing a book, even if that book is being published by a big publishing company. Printing presses—both the traditional offset kind and the new digital platforms—are most efficient when they are producing pages of words. Cost and complexity increase exponentially when you want colour illustrations. So it is worth asking, do you really need all these pictures? Can you get by with fewer? Can they be black and white rather than colour?

Remember: if you are going to publish photographs with people in them, it is most considerate to ask them beforehand if you can.

A special word for those who want to write a children's picture book. If you can't illustrate it yourself, you might want to consider co-writing with somebody who can. It can be very expensive to publish a colour children's picture book on your own, so this is a case where finding a small press publisher to work with might be advisable.

12

Other things that go in a book

You've read enough books to know that there are other things between the covers than just the stories. Here are some of the things you might need:

- Copyright information. This usually goes inside the front cover or on early pages and usually includes the copyright symbol (©), the year of publication, the name of the author, and the statement "All Rights Reserved".
- Dedication. Is there a particular person or group you want to dedicate the book to? This often goes on the first or second right hand page. You can phrase it however you want.
- Table of contents. Some books offer a table of contents for readers to find their way around the book. It goes at the start of the book and is arranged by sections and their page numbers.
- Index. An index can also be a good way for a reader to find their way around the book, but it goes at the back and is arranged alphabetically by idea.

- Acknowledgements. Plenty of people probably contributed support while you were writing your book. An acknowledgements page is a great place to say thank you publicly. This can go at the front or at the back, but directly after the last page of your story is the most common.
- About the author. Most books have some kind of biographical note about who wrote them; this can go in a few places: front, back, or inside the cover.

13

Check who has the copyright for the things in your book

If you came up with all the ideas in the book yourself and wrote it all by yourself, you probably don't need to worry about this. But do stop and think! Did you tell somebody else's story based on things they have told you? Make sure you have permission to write it, and have worked out with them how they want to be credited. Is it a collection of stories by other people that you have assembled and edited? Make sure you have a written agreement about how any income gets distributed, just in case it goes on to be a huge bestseller.

III

ALL ABOUT MONEY

14

Using the resources you have

Make a plan early on for how much you will spend as part of publishing your book. Because this can vary quite a lot, the first step is really to think about what resources you already have or could access: your savings, grants you could apply for, talented friends or family who might be able to help you reduce costs, and so on.

You can think about using pre-orders to finance production costs, or order a small batch of books first and use the money from selling those to finance another small batch of production.

'There was an ad in the paper for someone to record the oral history, and this is the old wording, of persons from non-English speaking backgrounds in Broken Hill...I did get that job. It was one of the most fulfilling things that I've ever done in my life. Interviewed over 70 people, and as I said, some of them were people that I knew...five copies I printed out of the PC and we hard bound those for the Multicultural Foundation of New South Wales and they actually provided the money for the [oral history] project...I think when we decided to publish, I don't think we did get a grant for the actual publishing of it, the printing of it. I think it might have been by people pre-ordering.' - Christine Adams, author of Sharing the Lode

'Well, people were asking us, where can we buy it? Where can we buy it? I thought, we'll have to get some more! First off, we gave away to the family. So then we had to find money to get the next edition financed. So that's what we do. We sell them off, and then we use the money to buy some more books.' — John Spencer, author of On Both Sides of the Fence

15

How much money do you actually make from self-publishing?

If you are hoping to make money from your publishing, it is definitely possible. The media sometimes has stories of self-published authors who become massive bestsellers, but this is very rare. What is more typical is that authors build up a large catalogue of self-published books and sell a small number of each which adds up to a regular income stream. To do this, you need to keep careful accounts and pay attention to the pricing of your book so that it both covers costs and meets the expectations of your readers.

The Australian Society of Authors reported on a global survey of 2000 self-published writers from around the world, and found they made about $20,000 per year. A Macquarie University study in Australia in 2022 found that traditionally published authors made about $18,800 per year. Obviously, there might be some people who make hundreds of thousands of dollars, and some people who make nothing at all.

16

Pricing your work

If you are making your book to sell rather than to give away, you will need to set a price for it. To do this, look at what other books cost of similar size and format in the genre of your title. Mass market trade fiction books, like romance and fantasy, are less expensive; large coffee table books or art books will necessarily cost more.

As part of your thinking, you also need to consider how much your books cost to produce to ensure you cover costs. If you are paying $50 per copy to print, then you need to sell them for at least that much or make a loss. If you are using a print on demand service the calculations will be different. IngramSpark offers a compensation calculation tool which is quite fun to use (google "publisher compensation calculator"). You enter all the variables for your book and it tells you how much profit or loss you will make on each copy. For example, I put in details for a 200 page, black and white paperback, set a price of $10, and it let me know I would make $2.83 profit on each one.

You will want to set the price quite a bit higher than the actual cost of making the book. This will mean you have added in allowances so that you can sell some copies at a discount to friends, families, bookstores or people buying multiple copies, and for payment processing fees and unexpected costs that might crop up. If this is part of how you make a living, you also want to include an allowance for your time and labour.

17

Payment processing for handselling copies: Square and Paypal

If you're selling a copy (or a few copies) of your book to an individual, you can accept cash, or you might want to set yourself up to receive card payments. This can be especially helpful if you are selling your books at a festival or a market. Two systems people often use are Square and Paypal. There are pros and cons of each (and you might decide to use both!).

With Paypal, people pay you using their phones. You could display a QR code to help people find your Paypal account on their phones. This can be an easy way to get paid fast, including from overseas, though Paypal takes quite a big fee for international payments. With Square, you buy a card swiper (not too expensive) and link it to a Square account, so people can use their physical cards to pay you. You have to pay Square a fee per month, but individual fees tend to be lower than Paypal and the interface is user friendly and reliable. Remember that another option is to direct people to online retailers that stock your book.

'[At markets] I would just give them a flyer and go, "Go to your favourite site and they'll post it to you." So you know, I did the flyers and talked about the books and I had one copy of each and then said, "Go online, you'll get a good deal. You'll get a better deal than I can do and it's all online." It's fabulous.' - Rose Siva

IV

MAKING THE BOOK

18

Imagining your book

Actually making the book begins with imagining it: what kind of a book do you want to create? Is it a large book with lots of photos, a small paperback, an easily accessible ebook, a hardcover with a ribbon bookmark, or a picture book with full colour illustrations? Once you have an imagined version of your book, that can guide your choices among all the different options for producing your book, which are described below. You might of course need to compromise on some aspects of your imagined book, depending on your budget.

'I would say there's something very different to a thing that's on a screen that you can share to a thing that you can hold...when they had that book, and they were walking around going, "This is mine, this is mine. Mine's on this page," and they could see their name in the front; that tangibility, that concrete thing, that it was out there in the world as physical object.' - Jane Vaughan, Big Sky Stories

'People can have it on their coffee table and say, oh I've got it, he's autographed it for me...I think the physical book is a good idea particularly for people who are not computer geeks.' - George Venables

'It's just been such an honour to witness how much love is flowing through those poems and pages and through the relationships that weave everybody into the interconnections that exist in this community. So that gives you a sense of how the book lives in the community and I think having it as a tangible paperback format, for people to hold and read and carry with them where they go is really important. Like you wouldn't have the same experience with ebook.' - Olivia Nigro from Running Water Community Press, publisher of Arelhekenhe Angkentye: Women's Talk poetry collection

19

Using a print shop

One straightforward way to turn your manuscript into a printed book is to use a printing shop, also just called a printer. You take your word document on a USB or email it to them, and they print out the pages and then bind them with a cover.

An advantage to using a print shop is that your business stays local and you can get to know the people printing your book. Some of the authors we've spoken to have received good advice from print shop staff about cover design and layouts for the book. Some print shops might be happy to let people who want a copy of your book order directly with them (a kind of 'print on demand' model). Usually, authors will order a box of 50 or 100 copies and then distribute these themselves.

Two disadvantages to printing your book at a print shop are that there are limited formatting options, and that they are more expensive than some options. The books probably will look a bit more homemade than books in a bookshop: the format will likely be A4 (or otherwise larger than typical books) and the paper is often glossy. Photos and images can be printed in full colour if you want. A book like that will probably cost between $35 and $50 per copy, which means you need to sell them at quite a high price to break even on costs.

'We had quite a few conversations [in the writing group] about what is the goal of this anthology, because I personally wanted to go with IngramSpark and get a cheaper copy so that we could get it around because the original intent was to use it as marketing for the group and get more people to join the group. But other people wanted to go with the local printer shop no matter the price.' — Megan Hippler

20

Submitting to a publisher

You might prefer to submit your manuscript to a publisher rather than launch into publishing it yourself. A publisher can certainly provide a lot of services (like editing, design and distribution, especially into bookstores - you should still expect to be involved in marketing as publishers often rely on authors for this). A publisher with a good reputation can also give your book a boost in terms of recognition.

If you want to submit to a publisher, you can look for lists of them online or check out the spines in a bookshop. It might also help if you have a personal connection to a publisher, through networking - for example meeting them at a writers festival. You will need to visit each publisher's website to find their instructions for submitting a manuscript, and your covering letter should explain why your book is a good fit for their company. Some established publishers will want you to have an agent first; the process for acquiring an agent is similar (look them up online and follow their instructions for submitting your manuscript). For agents and publishers, check to see that they are reputable, that they have no unexpected or complicated charges and fees, and that they have published a good range of previous books.

Don't be disheartened if publishers reject your submission. All publishers have to be very mindful of sales potential, so they will often reject a manuscript if there isn't an obvious and large market for the book. Lots of great and well-written books receive multiple rejections.

21

Sending your document to a printer or publishing services company

There are companies who will print and bind your manuscript for you, and send you a box of book copies. These might be printers of publishing services companies, where printing is one of the services. To find a company like this, you could ask someone you know for a referral, or search online. Be sure to read the customer reviews to ensure it's a reliable company that does quality work.

It did take courage to reach out for advice but it was always worth the effort! I did reach out to others in other Facebook groups...I would ask by saying, 'Look, this is a lot. Can anybody help me? Does anyone have any experience with publishing a book? Who did you use? How did you go about it?" - Sonya Bradley-Shoyer, author of Come...Walk With Me

22

Print on demand can really be worth the effort

Print on demand is a relatively new way of printing your books. For print on demand, you work with a website to upload your document and make decisions about the paper, cover and so on. The advantages of print on demand are that the quality is good and the price is usually quite cheap. You can also order very small amounts (even just one copy).

If you publish print on demand with a large company such as IngramSpark or Lulu.com, they will also keep information about your title in their database so that bookshops can order directly with them. You may also be able to distribute an ebook of your book through the same company so that it appears on sites like Booktopia (in Australia) or Amazon.

The main disadvantage of print on demand is that their websites can be quite complex with a lot of decisions to be made. There are several guides available to help you use the websites (eg google self-publishing with Ingram). It can really be worth it if you want your books to be affordable. For a book that Beth self-published with a friend, *The Frankfurt Kabuff*, she ordered a box of 50 copies and the books worked out at about $5 per copy.

'Having written, you then say, well what am I going
to do with this stuff. And it wasn't a terribly
arduous job to say, oh well, I think I'll go and give
IngramSpark a go. And that's what I've done, and 26
books later it still works.' – Denise Neville

23

The size of your book

The size of your book is something else to choose. When you are setting up at a print shop or for print or demand, they will ask you for "trim size" and will usually have quite a big range of options available. Usually, smaller sized books are cheaper to print. It can also be cheaper to pick an industry standard size rather than something bespoke.

If you are looking for a standard, medium-sized book, a "B-format" paperback (the one commonly used for novels) is 129 x 198mm in Australia (in the UK it is 130 x 197mm; it's OK to pick something close!). The "B plus format", sometimes used for non-fiction, is 135 x 210mm.

A "C-format" paperback is the larger paperback that you often see for new releases in Australia. Its size is 153 x 234mm. Mass-market fiction like romances and thrillers are sometimes printed in pocket-sized "A format" (110 x 178mm). Art books and coffee table books are larger and can vary in size.

Several of the self-published authors we spoke to chose larger formats for their books, usually because they wanted to include photos or because those were the options available at their print shop.

24

Paper type and cover type

At the printer or the website of a print on demand company, you'll be asked some questions about what kind of paper you want to use for the pages and the cover.

At IngramSpark for example the choices for paper are:

- Groundwood 38lb/56 gsm
- White 50lb/56gsm
- Crème 50lb/74 gsm
- White 70lb/74 gsm

You can google what these mean, but in essence the first word is the colour (not all whites are the same!) and the numbers refer to the weight of the paper (gsm is grams per square metre. The typical office paper is about 70gsm). Heavier paper is usually perceived as better quality, but it's more expensive and will also make the book itself heavier. Mass market fiction tends to use cheap paper. Cream paper can be easier on the eyes than white paper.

For the cover, you can also make choices. IngramSpark offers the choice between matte cover (soft feel, no shine) and gloss cover (high shine, smooth finish).

There are also choices about what kind of colour printing you might choose, and sometimes what kind of binding or glue you would like to use: the standard paperback uses perfect binding (glue).

25

Cover design

Designing a cover can be one of the most fun tasks in publishing your own book. You can use a free or paid computer program, or pay someone to design the cover for you. For ebooks, you need a front cover only. For print books, think about three parts: front cover, back cover, spine. You can design your cover on the computer (eg using Adobe or a free design program like Canva which has book cover templates). You will then need to export the file as a PDF or JPG for the printers. You can use your own photos, or look for royalty-free images online.

To get an idea of what's required, look at comparable books and analyse their covers. For the front cover: consider type elements, imagery, and current trends. Don't forget your name and your book title! For the back cover, be mindful to include standard elements including the ISBN, bar code, description of your book…more on these later).

For print books, choosing the size of your book will let you know how big the cover is. Knowing your trim size, paper type and the number of pages is important for working out the size of your spine. When Beth self-published with her friend Claire, they entered this information into the IngramSpark website and it gave them the spine width, which they needed to design the cover, and a PDF template to use as the basis for a design which included IngramSpark making the barcode for free. They edited the PDF template using Canva and Adobe then uploaded it to IngramSpark. They used photos they had taken themselves, so there was no need for copyright permissions.

26

Typesetting and layout

This section is about how to make your book look great inside as well as outside. A good interior book design makes a book pleasant to read, increasing reader engagement and enjoyment.

You can hire someone to do the typesetting of your manuscript, or do it yourself. If you are doing it yourself, start by looking at other books in the genre you are writing in to see how they are laid out inside. Try to replicate this – it will make for a smoother reading experience and more appealing book because it will seem familiar to readers. There are many online guides and free short courses that can teach you the basics of good layout.There are also free and paid computer programs that you can use to typeset your book. It is possible to typeset your book in Microsoft Word, however, it canbe tricky when it comes to publication and often does not help you to achieve a professional look. You can use the layout templates provided in IngramSpark if you are publishing on that platform. Another good typesetting website is Reedsy.

Some things to look out for when you are typesetting your book include how you will set out chapter headings, table of contents, and your font choices (see more below). You will need to be mindful of the amount of white space on the page, especially margins and gutters. Margins are the white space you leave around the text. Gutters are the margins on the inside of a book (where the fold is). Don't make these too small! Also look for stray lines of text left hanging at the top or bottom of a page. You can avoid these dangling lines by editing the text, or by leaving some extra blank space.

Once you have an interior layout for your book, you can export it as a PDF file and then send it to a printer or upload to a digital publishing platform.

27

What fonts should you choose?

Typically, you need two fonts for your book: one for headings, and one for the main text. Choose simple and readable fonts. For the main text, a serif font is a good choice. Serif fonts (which have strokes at the ends of the letters) are easier to read as blocks. Some examples of serif fonts are:

- Times New Roman
- Garamond
- Libre Caslon
- Georgia
- Palatino
- Adobe Minion

For headings, sans serif styles work well. Sans serif fonts are easier to read at large size and when they are just a few words. A sans serif font is also a good choice for the labels for any images.

Some examples of sans serif fonts are:

- Arial
- Helvetica
- Futura
- Geneva

The usual font size to use is 11pt for the body of your text (you could do 10pt or 12pt if you like the look of that better). Look at other published books in your genre for font ideas. The inside cover of books will often tell you what fonts they use. You might like to stay away from fonts that have become clichéd, such as Comic Sans and Papyrus. There are some people who get very passionate about fonts, and if that's your kind of creative expression there's lots of advice online that you can search for.

28

Formatting your images and photos for printing

For some books, images and photos in black and white or colour are really important – even if they add to the cost.

To help these images look as good as possible, you will want to pay attention to how they are formatted. Good image formats for printing are JPG, TIFF and PDF. You will want images to be quite high resolution - usually 300dpi (dots per inch) – so that they print crisply. Often small files can only be printed as small images. Getting high-quality digital scans of your photos somewhere like Officeworks can be a good idea to make sure the resolution is high enough to print well.

'At the launches that's something really beautiful to share is that people will take the book and sit in family groups and read it together. Be flicking through, looking at the photos.'- Olivia Nigro from Running Water Community Press, publisher of Living in Hope by Frank Byrne.

29

How many to print? Small editions are better than large editions

We've met a lot of writers whose garages store boxes of books they can't sell. We don't recommend you order a large amount of books up front, but how many is enough? Well, some larger printers will insist on a minimum print run, like 500 or 1000 books. In that case, always go with the minimum. Smaller printers, like the ones you might find in regional towns, may have a much lower minimum so do shop around. Books that sit in garages for a long time will eventually degrade (they get spotty and saggy), and then you won't be able to sell them. It's pretty heartbreaking to throw them in the recycling bin!

If you use print on demand like Ingram, you can print very small numbers, for example 50 at a time or even fewer. We know of authors who print 50, sell them, then use that money to print the next box of 50. Every time you go to reprint, you can fix typos and make small changes, then call the next batch a "second edition" (or third edition, etc).

30

Isbns and barcodes

To publish a book, whatever the format, you need an ISBN (International Standard Book Number). ISBNs are unique, 13 digit identifiers that are used to track your book in library and book ordering systems. We recommend you buy your own directly – it's not difficult, and many third party companies will charge a mark-up. In Australia you buy ISBNs online from Thorpe-Bowker. You need one for each format (for example, you will need separate ISBNs for paperback and ebook editions of your book). A good plan is to buy the pack of 10 they currently price at $88. There is also a set up fee for new publishers who have not bought an ISBN before (currently $55).

Print books will need a barcode. You can make one for free with an online barcode generator (search for one of these online). Some platforms (e.g. IngramSpark) provide you with a barcode when you use their distribution and printing service.

V

GETTING YOUR BOOK INTO PEOPLE'S HANDS: PLANS FOR DISTRIBUTION

31

What is distribution?

When a book is published by a traditional publisher, they will likely have a distribution agreement with a distribution company. The role of the distribution company is to get the books from the publisher's warehouse to different bookstores and libraries.

For DIY publishing, this can look a little different. If you are going to publish with a platform like IngramSpark or Amazon, they can handle some of the distribution for you (ebooks and print on demand), but you can also do some distribution yourself. Different platforms offer different services, so make sure you pick the one that most suits your publishing and distribution needs. If you avoid these platforms and get your book printed at the local printer, you will be responsible for getting your book into your readers' hands. There's more information on all these options in the sections following this one.

32

Getting into bookstores and libraries

When you publish your book independently, the best way to get it into bookstores and libraries is to develop relationships with booksellers and librarians and encourage them to stock your book.

Talk to staff at your local libraries about your book. They will most likely order from their library supplier. For this reason you should also aim to find out who their library supplier is, and upload information about your title to the library supplier's online portal. Some examples of library suppliers in Australia are James Bennett Pty Ltd and Peter Pal Library Supplier. Ideally do thisbeforethe book is published.

You can also establish relationships with staff at bookshops, other shops, and other points of sale. Some may buy 'on consignment' from the author, which means they will take some copies from you without paying for them upfront, and then give you the money when they sell copies. However some will prefer to order from a wholesaler. If your book is listed on a site such as Ingram, a retailer can order from them. However they are only likely to order the book when a sale to a customer has actually occurred (that is, the customer can ask them to order a copy, but the shop probably won't carry spare copies in their shop).

'A lot of these people who are self-published, I know it's going to be popular because of their relationships with town and the people and the communities ... I'll go, "okay, how would you like me to order it in?" And then I'll say, "Do you want me to order it through you," because sometimes that's what I have to do, or, "do you want to me to order maybe through Ingram" and then they don't have to worry about getting the books to me.' - Bronwyn Druce, bookseller at Red Kangaroo Books, Alice Springs.

33

Posting books through the mail

If you take orders online through your own website or via email (direct sales), you will need to pack and post each book yourself. It's worth considering what packing materials you need and buying in bulk. You will also want to keep a record of sales and dispatch.

34

Legal deposit

National and state libraries keep a record of every book published in Australia or the state, preserving books for future generations and building a picture of our culture. Having books in these libraries also helps people find your work.

If you publish your own book, you must deposit a copy with the National Library of Australia and your state or territory library. Each library only needs one copy. To find out more, visit library.gov.au where they have a whole section on legal deposit.

35

Ebook distribution

If you are doing an ebook as one of the formats for your book, it can be distributed to customers a number of ways. You might keep the ebook as a file (like a PDF) that you can email to people after they buy a copy from you (either from your own website or in person).

If you are doing print on demand with Ingram, you can click a button and they will also distribute the ebook to online retailers such as Amazon, Kobo and Booktopia. If you want to publish directly with Amazon (eg through their Kindle Direct Publishing program) you will be given the option to make the ebook available exclusively through Amazon. If this is where most of your customers are, it can be worth it because it lets you sell at a cheaper price and means your book is included in promotions on the site. Remember you will need a separate ISBN for the ebook version of your book.

VI

TELLING PEOPLE ABOUT YOUR BOOK: MARKETING

36

What is marketing?

If you want people to read your book, they'll have to find out that it exists. You can't tell everybody about it one at a time, so you need to think of ways of letting lots of readers know all at once.

You'll need to reflect on who the audience for your book is, and where they might get their news about books from. These two questions are things you can start thinking about even before you've finished writing. There might be things you can do while you're writing the book that can help build an audience, for example public speaking engagements on your topic or building a social media profile. Once your book is published, you can ramp up with specific strategies for promotion.

37

The blurb

A blurb is a short piece of writing (about 200-250 words) that goes on the back of a book and makes the reader want to peek inside. Your blurb actually has two important jobs: first, to make readers curious enough to open your book, and second, to help them find it in the first place – because blurbs are readable by search engines online, and also affect how bookstores might shelve it.

Let's start with making readers curious. Ask yourself: What would make someone want to spend time with your book? If you've written a military thriller, maybe it's your exotic setting or the technical detail of weapons and warfare. If it's a memoir about your years as a schoolteacher, perhaps it's the heartwarming stories of students whose lives you touched. Whatever makes your book special, that's what needs to shine in your blurb.

To get started, write down three things that make your book unique. Then jot down what feelings you want your reader to experience. Finally, think about similar books your readers might enjoy, and look at their blurbs. Remember, you don't need to tell the whole story – just enough to make them want to know more.

Blurbs are also useful for directing readers to your book. Think of the words in your blurb as signposts pointing the way to your book. If you've written a romance novel set in Cornwall, you'll want to naturally include words like "romance," "love story," and "Cornwall" in your blurb. These words are useful for how the book is sold: where a bookstore or library might place it, or how it might be grouped in an online bookstore. Blurbs can help what the industry calls 'discoverability'.

As an example, here is the blurb for Shaken not Stirred, written and published by Susie Sarah:

Jane Bund, turning 60, feels just a little shaken by the loss of her dearly-departed husband Freddy. Her new status as a senior brings on a desperate need to alleviate encroaching boredom. Leafing through the Sydney paper as she sips her latte, she comes across an article that changes her life forever. Enjoy the roller-coaster ride with Jane and her elderly friends as they take on ASIO and the CIA, proving that age is no barrier to learning new skills and having fun. Set in the sleepy seaside town of Paradise Cover on the Far South NSW Coast, this spy novel will entertain, intrigue and delight you.

38

Codes and keywords that help people discover your book

At some points in the publishing process you may need to choose codes or keywords for your book. Think of keywords as searchable terms that describe your book's content, themes, and genre. You'll need at least three strong keywords, but more is better. For example, if you've written a mystery set in a bakery, your keywords might include "cosy mystery," "culinary mystery," "amateur sleuth," "small town," and "bakery." These keywords help your book appear in searches when readers are looking for similar stories.

The publishing industry uses two main systems to categorize books: BISAC (in North America) and Thema (internationally). These are standardized codes that tell booksellers and libraries exactly where your book belongs. While you don't need to memorize these systems, you should familiarize yourself with the main categories that fit your book. Your publisher or self-publishing platform will help you select the right codes.

To choose effective keywords, try:

- Looking at similar books in your genre to see what terms they use
- Using Google's search suggestions to find popular related terms
- Checking Amazon's category system
- Using AI tools to research trending terms in your genre

Remember that your keywords work together with your book cover and blurb as a complete marketing package. These elements should align - if your keywords suggest a romance novel but your cover looks like a thriller, readers will be confused.

39

Professional author photos and bios (aka you as a "brand")

Your author photo should be a high-quality headshot that presents you as approachable and professional. Wear clothes in solid colours that won't distract from your face. The photo should be well-lit and clearly show your features. You don't need to pay a photographer, but this shouldn't be a selfie. Get somebody to take the photo for you. Often it's best to take a lot of different shots then choose from among them.

Your author biography should be a short, engaging paragraph that connects with your book's genre. Write it in the third person, highlighting relevant experience or interests that relate to your writing. Think about what your readers would find interesting about you.

Consider creating a simple author website using services like WordPress or Wix. This gives readers a place to learn about your book and find purchase links. Remember to keep any online presence current. An outdated website or dormant social media account can work against you, so it's better to maintain one active platform well than several poorly.

Think of these elements as your professional writing wardrobe - they should make you feel confident while authentically representing who you are as an author. That authentic connection between your self and your book is your author brand.

40

A press release for your book

A press release is a powerful tool for spreading the word about your book, and it's simpler than you might think. Keep it to one page and make it newsworthy - perhaps focus on your local connection, an interesting aspect of your research, or a timely topic your book addresses.

Start with a compelling headline and opening paragraph that includes the essential information: your book's title, genre, release date and a hook that makes your story interesting. Follow this with a brief description of your book, a short quote from you about what inspired it, and your relevant background or expertise.

Always include high-quality images with your press release - both your book cover and your professional author photo. These should be high-resolution files suitable for print (300 dpi). Make it easy for media outlets to use your material by providing everything they need in one package.

Research local newspapers, magazines, blogs and podcasts that might be interested in your book. Look for those that cover local authors or your book's subject matter. Create a simple spreadsheet to track your media contacts and communications. When you reach out, personalise each message and be clear about why their audience would be interested in your story.

Keep your media contacts updated about launch events, book-shop signings or other newsworthy developments. Remember, local media often appreciate stories about local authors - you're part of their community's story.

41

Use your friends to boost your signal

Don't underestimate the power of endorsements and word-of-mouth promotion for your book. A thoughtful endorsement from someone respected in your field can catch readers' eyes and build credibility. While approaching people for endorsements might feel daunting, be professional and direct: send a polished manuscript, clear deadline, and specific request about the length of endorsement you need.

Look beyond famous names - consider approaching local experts, community leaders, or specialists in your book's subject matter. A genuine endorsement from someone with real connection to your topic can be more valuable than a generic one from a bigger name.

Your personal networks are equally powerful marketing tools. Share your publishing journey with friends, family and colleagues. Use your existing connections creatively. If you're part of a sports club, church group or professional network, these communities can become enthusiastic supporters of your work. Word-of-mouth recommendations from trusted friends are still one of the most effective ways to find new readers.

42

Promoting your book on social media

Choose social media platforms where your target readers actually spend time. If you've written a cookbook, visual platforms like Instagram or Pinterest might work best. For fiction, you might find more engagement on Facebook. Build genuine connections by joining online communities that match your book's subject or genre. This might be Facebook groups about gardening for your horticultural guide, or Goodreads groups for your genre of fiction. Participate in discussions, share your expertise, and be a genuine member of these communities - not just someone promoting their book.

Remember that other authors aren't your main audience. While writing communities are supportive, focus your energy on connecting with actual readers. Look for book clubs, subject-interest groups, and topic-specific forums where your potential readers gather. Start building these connections well before your book launches. Share interesting aspects of your writing journey, respond to comments, and engage with others' posts. When it comes time to promote your book, you'll have an established presence and supportive network rather than appearing just to sell.

Don't just post about your book - share content your target readers would find interesting. This might be insights about your research, related news articles, or behind-the-scenes glimpses of your writing process. The goal is to be an engaging presence, not a continuous advertisement.

43

Promoting your book on a newsletter

Building an email list is one of the most effective ways to maintain a direct connection with your readers. Unlike social media, where your posts might get lost in the algorithm, email lets you reach your readers directly. Start collecting email addresses early - add a simple sign-up form to your website, offer it at events, and mention it in your book's back matter. Consider offering something special to encourage sign-ups, like a free short story or exclusive content related to your book.

Keep in touch regularly, but don't overwhelm your subscribers. A monthly or quarterly newsletter is plenty. Share news about your writing, upcoming events, and personal insights into your creative process. Remember, these are people who've chosen to hear from you - make your communications personal and valuable. Most importantly, treat your email list with respect. Never share subscribers' details, and make it easy for people to unsubscribe if they wish. Services like Substack, MailChimp or TinyLetter can help you manage your list professionally and legally.

44

Promoting your book at events

Participating in book fairs, writers' festivals and literary events can be rewarding, but requires careful planning to make it worth your investment. Before committing to an event, consider both the costs and potential benefits. Calculate all expenses: registration fees, travel, accommodation, meals, and the cost of books you'll need to bring. Some events charge substantial fees for trade tables or exhibition space. Consider whether you're likely to sell enough books to cover these costs, or whether the networking and exposure opportunities justify the expense. Some events have a bookseller in attendance, and you will need to work out a profit-sharing arrangement with them. If you are selling your own books, have plenty on hand, clear pricing displayed, and consider accepting card payments.

Take advantage of any additional opportunities the event offers, such as speaking slots, panel discussions or reading sessions. These can help you reach more potential readers and add value to your attendance beyond direct sales.

45

Promoting your book at libraries and bookshops

When approaching libraries, offer to do an author talk or reading. Many libraries are keen to support local authors and can help promote your event to their community. Some might also purchase copies for their collection. Build relationships with library staff - they often recommend books to readers and host book clubs.

Bookshops and other local retailers often welcome opportunities to support local authors. Consider consignment arrangements where they stock a few copies of your book and pay you when they sell. Make it easy for them by providing clear pricing information and professional point-of-sale materials like posters or bookmarks.

Think creatively about where your potential readers might be - tourist information centres, museums, craft shops, local markets, agricultural shows, and community events can be excellent places to showcase your work. These venues sometimes have stall spaces where you can sell directly to readers. While some events require investment in terms of stall fees and your time, they're excellent opportunities to meet readers face-to-face and build word-of-mouth promotion.

Consider setting aside a portion of your books for promotional copies. While giving away books might seem counterintuitive, strategic gifting to key community members, reviewers, or potential bulk buyers can lead to valuable exposure and sales opportunities. Keep track of these promotional copies and follow up politely to maintain these important local connections.

46

Holding a book launch

A book launch is an exciting way to celebrate your achievement and kick-start sales. While launches can be elaborate affairs, a simple, well-planned event can be just as effective and much less stressful.

Consider approaching your local independent bookshop, library, community centre, or even a favourite café. Choose somewhere easily accessible with enough space for people to mingle comfortably. Light refreshments help create a welcoming atmosphere. Keep it simple - wine, soft drinks, and some light snacks are plenty. Ask a friend to manage the refreshments so you can focus on your guests.

Plan for about an hour of formal proceedings. You'll want to include a short reading from your book (practise this beforehand!), perhaps a brief talk about what inspired you to write it, and time for questions from the audience. Arrange for someone to introduce you - this could be a friend, local writer, or bookshop owner.

Make it easy for people to buy your book. If you're not in a bookshop, bring plenty of copies and have a clearly marked sales table. Consider having a card reader available for payments. Have a pen ready - people often enjoy getting their copies signed.

Most importantly, invite plenty of people! Send invitations about three weeks ahead, use social media, and ask friends to spread the word. Local media might be interested too. Remember, a launch isn't just about sales - it's a chance to thank your supporters and celebrate your achievement.

```
'Because we were doing a book launch ... they printed
in hyper-speed and brought them out, and we got to
gift one to all of the participants, which was really
excellent, but then we had extras that they could
buy, and there were lots of parents and grandparents
who were very excited to send one off to Grandma and
do all that kind of thing ... it was just super cool.
And then everyone was walking around going, "Will you
sign my book for me?" it was amazingly beautiful,
lovely.' — Jane Vaughan, Big Sky Stories, coordinator
of the anthology Campaign to Sky's End: Quests and
Tales from the Youth of Far West NSW
```

VII

APPENDICES: STUFF IT'S GOOD TO KNOW

47

Publishing Glossary

Backmatter: All material in the book that follows the main text, including appendices, glossary, bibliography, index, and acknowledgements.

Barcode: A machine-readable "zebra" pattern of your ISBN, required on the back cover of print books so it can be scanned for sale in book shops.

BISAC/Thema codes: The standard subject classifications used by the book industry to categorise books. These help people find books in stores and online.

Blurb: A short promotional description of the book (typically 200-250 words) that appears on the back cover or online listings, designed to entice readers to purchase the book.

CMYK: The colour model used in printing (Cyan, Magenta, Yellow, and Key/Black), in contrast to the RGB model (Red, Green, Blue) used for digital displays.

Consignment: An arrangement with a bookshop, where they stock your book with no up-front payment. Instead, they pay you once copies are sold.

Copy-editing: A detailed edit focusing on grammar, spelling, punctuation, consistency, and stylistic improvements at the sentence level .

Distribution: The process of getting books to shops and other places that might sell them.

DPI (Dots Per Inch): A measurement of image resolution; 300 DPI is typically required for high-quality print publication.

Frontmatter: All material before the main text of the book, including title page, copyright page, dedication, table of contents, and preface.

GSM (Grams per Square Metre): Measurement of paper weight; higher GSM indicates thicker, heavier paper. Typical book paper ranges from 70-120 GSM.

Gutter: The inner margin of a book page, where it meets the binding. Needs to be wider than other margins to ensure text isn't lost in the fold.

InDesign: Professional software commonly used for book layout and typesetting.

ISBN (International Standard Book Number): A unique 13-digit identifier assigned to each edition of a book. Required for commercial distribution, cataloguing, and tracking sales. In Australia, these are purchased from Thorpe-Bowker.

Legal deposit: A legal requirement to provide one copy of your published book to the National Library of Australia and your state or territory library for preservation.

Metadata: Information about your book (title, author, description, categories, etc.) that helps readers discover it in searches and online retailers.

Perfect binding: The standard method for paperback binding where pages are glued to the spine and cover, creating a flat, squared spine.

POD (Print on Demand): A digital printing technology where books are printed individually or in small batches as orders are received, eliminating the need for large print runs and warehouse storage.

Proofreading: This is your final quality check before publication, catching any remaining typos, grammatical errors, formatting inconsistencies or layout problems.

Royalties: The percentage of money from each sale that is paid to the author. In self-publishing of print books, authors typically receive 100% of profits after production and distribution costs.

Sans serif fonts: Typefaces without decorative lines at the ends of letter strokes, often used for headings and display text (e.g., Arial, Helvetica).

Serif fonts: Typefaces with small decorative lines (serifs) at the ends of letter strokes, typically used for body text as they guide the eye along lines of text (e.g., Times New Roman, Garamond).

Structural editing: Big-picture editing that takes an overview of the book, offering suggestions on the overall organisation and flow of a manuscript. A structural edit might address issues like pacing, character development, or argument structure.

Trim size: The final dimensions of a book after printing and cutting. Standard trim sizes include B-format (129 x 198mm in Australia) and C-format (153 x 234mm).

Typesetting: The process of arranging text and images on the page to create a visually appealing, readable book layout, including considerations like font selection, margins, and spacing.

Vanity publishing: Publishing services that charge authors high fees for publication with minimal quality control and marketing support, and that may be predatory (see next section below).

48

How to spot a predatory company

There are predatory companies associated with publishing. These companies often target first time authors, and they may run competitions or prizes too. They charge a lot of money (thousands of dollars) in one bulk sum, and often keep control over your files and online passwords associated with your book so you cannot reprint them yourself. They make little effort to market your book and often only print a few copies. Predatory publishing is sometimes also known as vanity publishing.

To avoid falling prey to one of these unscrupulous companies, there are several things you can do. First, be suspicious. If a company's ads follow you around the internet, or they are persistent in emailing or calling you, they are likely to be at the very least expensive if not predatory.

Second, research companies thoroughly first to see what other authors'experiences have been like. You might find reviews through Google, Reddit or Facebook groups. You can also check out the Alliance of Independent Authors' Watchdog List.This is time consuming but well worth the effort in saving you from paying too much for a book that is not what you want.

Third, know your rights. There are government websites (these end in .gov.au in Australia) that can advise you about your consumer rights and some include specific information about predatory publishing.

It is always good practice to double or triple check any source you use.In this guide, we have collated resources from various places but we haven't reviewed them in depth. Please make sure you Google search anyone who claims to be an expert, especially if they are asking you for money.

> 'The big problem is that since I've brought the book
> out [with Xlibris] I have received so many emails
> from other publishers and people from all over the
> place, America, saying, you know, you've published a
> book, do you want to publish your next book through
> us? And it's a bit painful. I just delete them now.
> And phone calls.' — Marilyn Harris, author of Dust
> and Drama

About the authors

Beth Driscoll is Professor in Publishing and Communications and Deputy Dean Academic in the Faculty of Arts at the University of Melbourne. She teaches in the Master of Publishing and Communications. She is the author of *What Readers Do* (Bloomsbury Academic, 2024) and co-author with Kim Wilkins and Lisa Fletcher of *Genre Worlds: Popular Fiction in Twenty-First Century Book Culture* (University of Massachusetts Press, 2022). She has also self-published fiction with her collaborator Claire Squires, under the nom-de-plume Blaire Squiscoll (*The Frankfurt Kabuff* and *Tante Fran's May 68 Book Club: Choose Your Own Revolution*)

Kim Wilkins is a Professor of Writing, and Associate Dean (Research) of Humanities, Arts, and Social Sciences at the University of Queensland. She has published scholarship relating to genre fiction, bestsellers, and book culture. She is also the author of more than 30 works of fiction and has her works translated into more than 20 languages. Her novel *Wildflower Hill* (written as Kimberley Freeman) was a Target Book Club pick in the United States.

Alexandra Dane is a Senior Lecturer in Media and Communications. Her research focuses on the production and circulation of power in contemporary book cultures. She is the author of

White Literary Taste Production in Contemporary Book Culture (2023, Cambridge UP).

Professor Sandra Phillips has extensive industry experience as a former publisher and editor, and is Professor of Publishing and Communications at the University of Melbourne. As Associate Dean Indigenous, Professor Sandra Phillips leads Indigenous strategy for impact across the Faculty of Arts at the University of Melbourne. A Wakka Wakka and Gooreng Gooreng mother and grandmother, Sandra's research also includes the Reading Climate: Indigenous Literatures, School English, and Sustainability project.